Adult
Life Skills
for
Older Teens

The Practical Guide for Older Teens to Learn Money
Management, Cooking, Fitness, and Healthy Eating:
Navigating the Transition to Adulthood..

Adam N. Worthy

TABLE OF CONTENTS

CHAPTER 5
Basic Home Maintenance and Repairs
Understanding basic home systems
DIY repairs and safety measures
Hiring professionals

CHAPTER 6
Cooking and Nutrition
Meal planning and preparation
Understanding nutritional needs
Kitchen safety

CHAPTER 7
Self-care and Personal Hygiene
Importance of self-care
Developing a personal care routine
Maintaining personal hygiene

CHAPTER 8
Building and Maintaining Healthy Relationships
Understanding the importance of relationships
Effective communication skills
Conflict resolution

CHAPTER 9
Independent Living Skills
Preparing for independent living
Essential life skills
Problem-solving and decision making

CHAPTER 10
Civic Engagement and Social Responsibility
Understanding civic engagement
Volunteering and community service
Building social awareness and responsibility.

CHAPTER 1

Introduction: Importance of Adult Life Skills for Older Teens

Introduction:

The transition to maturity may be a stressful period for older teenagers as they begin to take on greater responsibility and independence. Developing adult life skills is vital for their success and well-being during this period.

In this chapter, we'll discuss the relevance of adult life skills for older teenagers and how learning these abilities may enable them to be more prepared for the real world.

What are Adult Life Skills?

Adult life skills relate to the talents and knowledge required to manage and take care of oneself and one's duties as an adult. These skills include budgeting and financial management, time management and organization, job hunting and resume building, basic home maintenance and repairs, cooking and nutrition, self-care and personal hygiene, building and maintaining healthy relationships, communication skills, and civic engagement and social responsibility.

Why are Adult Life Skills Important for Older Teens?

Older teenagers are at a vital point in their life as they prepare to reach adulthood and become independent. Adult life skills are vital for their success and well-being throughout this transition time. These abilities empower older teenagers with the knowledge and capacity to handle their obligations, make smart choices, and become self-sufficient and independent adults.

By acquiring and mastering these abilities, older teenagers will be better equipped to tackle the difficulties of the real world and have a higher chance of attaining success in their personal and professional life.

Budgeting and Financial Management:
One of the most crucial adult life skills for older teenagers to acquire is budgeting and money management. Understanding how to build and keep to a budget, and understanding the foundations of personal economics, are crucial for controlling spending and making sensible financial choices.

Additionally, saving and investing for the future is vital to develop a solid financial foundation that will set them up for success in the long term.

Time Management and Organization:
Effective time management and organizing skills are equally vital for older teenagers to master. These abilities help older kids prioritize work, fulfill deadlines, and manage their obligations efficiently. It will also enable them to minimize stress, keep on top of their job, and ultimately be more productive.

Job Hunting and Resume Building:
As older kids approach maturity, they'll need to start thinking about getting a job and joining the workforce. Job-seeking and CV-building skills are vital for older kids to locate acceptable work, increase their employability, and raise their chances of getting a job.

Other Adult Life Skills:
Other adult life skills such as basic house maintenance and repairs, cooking and nutrition, self-care and personal hygiene, and creating and sustaining healthy relationships which all will be explored in full in the coming chapters

CHAPTER 2

Budgeting and Financial Management

Budgeting and money management are critical life skills that are vital for older kids to acquire as they prepare for adulthood and independence. Teaching budgeting and financial management skills to older kids may help them make the most of their money, control spending, and prepare for future financial issues.

In this chapter , we'll cover the significance of budgeting and money management for older teenagers and present practical advice and techniques for helping them acquire these abilities.

Why is budgeting and money management crucial for older teens?

As older kids begin to take on more responsibility and independence, they must grasp how to handle their money and spending.

Budgeting and financial management skills can assist individuals to make the most of their money, minimizing needless spending, and preparing for the future.

Additionally, having a firm grasp of personal finance may enable older kids to make sensible financial choices and avoid financial traps later in life.

How can older teenagers acquire budgeting and money management skills?

There are various methods that older kids may acquire budgeting and money management skills:

- Lead by example: Parents and guardians may set a positive example by budgeting and managing their funds efficiently. This may give older kids a helpful role model and a personal experience in budgeting and money management.

- Educate them: Provide older teenagers with educational tools, such as books and websites, that teach budgeting and money management topics in an easy-to-understand fashion.

- Build a budget: Work with older kids to create a budget that takes into account their income and spending. This will allow students to understand the significance of budgeting and how to handle their money properly.

- Provide an allowance: Provide older teenagers with an allowance, and educate them on how to handle money properly by establishing spending restrictions and encouraging them to save a part of their allowance.

- Get a bank account: Encourage older adolescents to open a bank account, and educate them on how to use it properly by setting spending restrictions and encouraging them to save a part of their allowance.

- Give them money obligations: Assign older teenagers with financial responsibilities, such as paying for their wardrobe or mobile phone charges. This will assist children to understand the significance of budgeting and money management in real-life situations.

By following these steps, older teenagers may gain the budgeting and money management skills they need to be successful in the future.

Creating a budget, adhering to it, and saving and investing are critical parts of efficient budgeting and financial management. For older teens, knowing how to budget, save, and invest is particularly vital as they begin to take on more responsibility and independence.

we'll discuss tactics for building a budget, recommendations for keeping to your budget, and ways for older teens to start saving and investing for the future.

CREATING A BUDGET:

Creating a budget is the first step in managing your money properly. The method may be simplified by splitting it down into three steps:

- Determine your income: This includes any money you earn through allowances, part-time work, or any other sources.

- Identify your expenses: Make a list of all of your normal costs, such as allowance, entertainment, transportation, etc.

- Compare your income and expenditures: Compare your income and expenses to discover whether you are spending more than you are making.

If you are spending more than you are making, you'll need to make modifications to your budget to balance it out.

TIPS FOR STICKING TO YOUR BUDGET

Creating a budget is a vital step in managing money, but adhering to it may be difficult. For older teens, understanding how to keep to a budget is a key life skill as they begin to take on more responsibility and independence. Some advice and tactics for helping older adolescents keep to their budgets.

Tips for staying within your budget:

- Make a plan: Having a strategy in place might help you stay within your budget. Set precise objectives for what you want to do with your money, and develop a strategy for how you will achieve them.

- Track your spending: Keep track of all your costs, it will help you find trends and areas where you may be overpaying.

- Be realistic: Be realistic about what you can afford and what you need. Prioritize your expenditures by looking at what is important and what is not.

- Avoid impulsive purchasing: It is easy to get caught up in impulse shopping, but it is crucial to remember that every purchase you make should be thought out and prepared for.

SAVING AND INVESTING

Saving and investing are vital components of financial management, and older adolescents must learn about them as they begin to take on more responsibility and independence. Highlighting the significance of saving and investing for older teens, and share advice and techniques for helping them develop these abilities.

Why is saving and investing crucial for older teens?

Saving and investing is crucial for older adolescents because they assist them to prepare for their future financial objectives. Saving helps older adolescents to lay away money for future costs, such as school, a vehicle, or a down payment on a house. Investing, on the other hand, enables older teens to increase their money over time and generate wealth. Both of these actions are vital for establishing long-term financial stability.

How can older teens learn about saving and investing?

- Set financial goals: Having a defined financial objective may make saving and investing more manageable.

For example, older teens may desire to save money for a future purchase or invest money in a college savings account.

- Start a savings account: Encourage older teens to open a savings account and set up automatic transfers from their checking account to make saving simpler.

- Start modestly: Older teens need to start small and build their savings and investment amounts over time.

- Learn about various savings and investment alternatives: Older teens should educate themselves about numerous savings and investing options such as savings accounts, certificates of deposit, and mutual funds.

- Look for incentives: Many financial institutions provide rewards for establishing a savings account or beginning to invest.

Look for these incentives and take advantage of them.

- Get help: older teens might seek the counsel of a financial professional, or seek guidance from people that have the knowledge

CHAPTER 3

Time Management and Organization

Time management and organizing are critical life skills that are vital for older adolescents to acquire as they begin to take on more responsibility and independence. In this chapter , we will explore the significance of time management, suggestions for remaining organized, and tactics for prioritizing chores for older teenagers.

IMPORTANCE OF TIME MANAGEMENT:

Time management is a critical ability for older adolescents to acquire as they begin to balance schooling, extracurricular activities, and other obligations. Effective time management assists older adolescents to prioritize activities, fulfilling deadlines, and handling their obligations successfully.

This may assist to decrease stress, boost productivity, and improve general well-being.

TIPS FOR STAYING ORGANIZED:

- Use a planner or calendar: A planner or calendar might assist older teens to keep track of their schedule and deadlines.

- Keep a tidy office: A clean and organized workspace may assist older teens to remain focused and eliminate distractions.

- Create to-do lists: Creating a to-do list might assist older teens to prioritize chores and keep on track.

- Set aside a particular time for studying: Scheduling devoted study time might assist older teens to keep on top of their academics.

- Break down major chores into smaller ones: Breaking down enormous jobs into smaller, manageable portions may enable older teens to remain organized and make progress.

STRATEGIES FOR PRIORITIZING TASKS

For older teenagers, managing time and priorities are vital as they begin to take on greater responsibility and independence. Examining ways for prioritizing work that may assist older teenagers in keeping organized, minimizing stress, and making the most of their time.

- Understand your priorities: Start by deciding what is most essential to you, then concentrate on these priorities first.

- Use a To-Do List: Create a to-do list of chores that need to be performed. It's a wonderful visual reminder of what needs to be done and the option to mark off chores as they are accomplished will offer a feeling of success.

- Break down major jobs into smaller ones: Large projects may be intimidating and it can be hard to know where to begin. By breaking things down into smaller, manageable bits, older teens may make progress and observe the progress they have made.

- Use the Eisenhower Matrix: The Eisenhower matrix is a way of classifying jobs depending on their degree of significance and urgency. Older teenagers may utilize this strategy to prioritize tasks and concentrate on the most critical and urgent things first.

- Learn to say no: Older teenagers must learn how to say no to non-essential duties and demands, to concentrate on more critical concerns.

- Learn to handle distractions: Distractions may easily throw off a schedule and create delays in finishing work. Older kids may learn to detect and handle distractions to remain on track.

- Prioritize self-care: Taking care of oneself is crucial for general well-being, and should be incorporated as a priority to be able to perform effectively in other areas.

Overall, efficient time management and prioritizing tactics may enable older teenagers to remain organized, minimize stress, and make the most of their time.

By mastering these abilities and utilizing them frequently, older teens may better manage their obligations and accomplish their objectives.

CHAPTER 4

JOB HUNTING AND RESUME BUILDING

As older kids start to think about their future jobs, job seeking and CV preparation become vital life skills to acquire. In this page, we will explore acquiring work skills, producing a CV, and interviewing tactics that may enable older teens to stand out in the job market and secure the job they desire.

BUILDING JOB SKILLS:

- Volunteer: Participating in volunteer work may offer older kids useful experience and skills that are desired by employers.

- Get a part-time job: Having a part-time job may offer older kids essential work experience, and assist them to develop critical skills such as time management, communication, and collaboration.

- Attend relevant courses: Older teenagers may take classes in areas that are related to their future jobs, such as business, computer science, or communications.

- Learn a new skill: Taking the initiative to learn new talents, such as coding, graphic design, or social media marketing, may enable older teens to stand out in the employment market.

WRITING A RESUME:

- Personalize your CV to the job: Older teens should tailor their resumes to the exact job they are seeking, showcasing relevant skills and experiences.

- Use action verbs: Use action verbs to express your experience and abilities, such as "managed," "coordinated," or "developed."

- Keep it concise: A resume should be one or two pages, and older kids should concentrate on the most crucial material.

Check: Make careful to proofread the resume for any spelling or punctuation problems.

INTERVIEWING TIPS:

- Investigate the firm: Before an interview, older adolescents should research the company and the position they are looking for to demonstrate that they are interested in the job.

- Prepare responses to frequent interview questions: Prepare responses to popular interview questions such as "Why do you want to work here?" and "What are your strengths and weaknesses?"

- Dress properly: Older teens should dress professionally for an interview, since the way they show themselves is vital.

- Follow up: After the interview, older teens should follow up with a thank you message or email.

By mastering these job-seeking and CV-making skills, older teens may be more prepared for the job market, and boost their chances of finding the job they desire.

They may utilize the suggestions and tactics to exhibit their abilities and expertise, and create a fantastic impression on prospects

CHAPTER 5

BASIC HOME MAINTENANCE AND REPAIRS

As older kids start to take on more responsibility and independence, learning basic house maintenance and repair skills may be incredibly useful. In this page, we will address understanding fundamental house systems, DIY repairs and safety measures, and when to engage specialists for older adolescents.

UNDERSTANDING BASIC HOME SYSTEMS:

- Electrical: Learn about fundamental electrical systems and how to solve typical problems such as circuit breaker tripping or flickering lights.

- Plumbing: Learn about fundamental plumbing systems and how to handle typical problems such as blocked drains or leaking faucets.

- HVAC: Learn about fundamental heating, ventilation, and air conditioning systems and how to troubleshoot typical difficulties such as a furnace not functioning or a loud air conditioner.

DIY Repairs and Safety Measures:

- Safety first: Always emphasize safety while undertaking DIY repairs, and understand the dangers connected with particular jobs.

- Gather the proper tools: Have the correct tools on hand before beginning a repair, and use them carefully to prevent mishaps.

- Learn from experts: Watch online courses or read articles on house repairs to acquire the appropriate approaches.

- Know your limits: Understand your limits and don't pursue projects that are beyond your skills.

HIRING PROFESSIONALS

As older teens start to take on more responsibility and independence, understanding when and how to employ specialists for house maintenance and repairs may be a vital life skill. In this chapter , we will explore the significance of employing specialists for particular activities, how to research and compare possible contractors, and advice for dealing with professionals to achieve a good conclusion.

Why Hire Professionals?

- Safety: Some repairs and maintenance operations may be harmful and should only be undertaken by skilled specialists to guarantee safety.

- Expertise: Professionals have the expertise, skills, and experience to handle repairs and maintenance operations effectively and efficiently.

- Warranties: Many specialists provide guarantees for their services, which may give you peace of mind and protection in case anything goes wrong.

RESEARCHING AND COMPARING PROFESSIONALS:

- Ask for references: Ask friends, family, and neighbors for referrals to competent experts.

- Check credentials: Make sure the expert you employ is licensed, bonded, and insured.

- Read reviews: Look for internet reviews and ratings to obtain a sense of the professional's reputation and quality of work.

- Get several estimates: Get quotations from various experts to compare pricing and services provided.

Working with Professionals:

- Communicate clearly: Convey your requirements and expectations to the expert to ensure they grasp the extent of the project.

- Get everything in writing: Make sure you receive a formal estimate and contract that details the extent of the project, materials and labor prices, and any guarantees given.

- Ask questions: Don't be hesitant to ask questions and explain any issues you may have.

- Inspect the work: Inspect the work done by the expert to verify it fulfills your expectations and is done to a high quality.

By recognizing the necessity of hiring specialists, researching and comparing possible contractors, and successfully interacting with them, older teens may assure a good conclusion for house maintenance and repair jobs. This may save them time, and money and guarantee safety for themselves and their family.

CHAPTER 6

COOKING AND NUTRITION

As older teenagers start to take on more responsibility and independence, acquiring basic culinary and nutrition skills may be a crucial life skill.

Exploring meal planning and preparation, recognizing nutritional requirements, and kitchen safety for older teenagers.

MEAL PLANNING AND PREPARATION:

- Plan your meals: Plan your meals, and develop a shopping list of the goods you'll need.

- Learn fundamental culinary methods: Learn basic cooking techniques such as chopping, sautéing, and baking to increase your recipe possibilities.

- Experiment with new recipes: Experiment with different dishes and ingredients to extend your culinary horizons.

- Cook in quantity: Cook in bulk and freeze leftovers for fast and simple dinners on busy days.

UNDERSTANDING NUTRITIONAL NEEDS:

- Learn about macronutrients and micronutrients: Understand the significance of macronutrients like carbs, proteins, and fats, as well as micronutrients like vitamins and minerals.

- Learn about food groups: Understand the main food types and their nutritional advantages.

- Read labels: Learn how to read food labels and comprehend the ingredients and nutritional information.

- Consult a registered nutritionist or physician: Consult with a trained dietitian or physician to understand your dietary requirements.

KITCHEN SAFETY:

- Understand kitchen dangers: Understand typical kitchen hazards such as knife cuts, burns, and food poisoning.

- Keep a clean kitchen: Keep a clean kitchen to lessen the danger of food poisoning and other risks.

- Use good cooking procedures: Use proper cooking techniques to limit the risk of burns and other accidents.

- Use the correct tools: Use the right tools for the work and use them properly to limit the chance of harm.

By acquiring basic culinary and nutrition skills, older teens may take charge of their health and well-being. They can plan and prepare nutritious meals, assess nutritional requirements, and practice kitchen safety to guarantee a safe and happy cooking experience.

CHAPTER 7

SELF-CARE AND PERSONAL HYGIENE

As older teenagers start to take on more responsibility and independence, knowing about self-care and personal hygiene is a vital life skill. In this page, we will explore the significance of self-care, building a personal care regimen, and maintaining personal hygiene for older teenagers.

IMPORTANCE OF SELF-CARE:

- Physical and emotional well-being: Self-care is vital for preserving physical and emotional well-being.

- Stress management: Self-care methods such as exercise, meditation, and relaxation may assist older teenagers to handle stress.

- Positive body image: Self-care may enable older teens to develop a positive body image and self-esteem.

DEVELOPING A PERSONAL CARE ROUTINE:

- Start with the basics: Begin with the fundamentals such as brushing your teeth and washing your face in the morning and before night.

- Identify particular requirements: Identify specific needs such as skincare or hair care, and include them in the regimen.

- Make it a habit: Make self-care a habit by integrating it into a routine.

- Experiment: Experiment with various self-care routines, such as yoga or writing, to determine what works best for you.

MAINTAINING PERSONAL HYGIENE:

- Daily washing/bathing: Regular showering or bathing is crucial for maintaining personal hygiene.

- Brushing and flossing: Brush and floss at least twice a day to maintain dental hygiene.

- Washing hands: Regularly washing hands may help reduce the spread of germs and sickness.

- Grooming: Regularly groom hair, nails, and body hair as appropriate.

CHAPTER 8

BUILDING AND MAINTAINING HEALTHY
RELATIONSHIPS

As older kids learn to navigate through varied
social situations, creating and sustaining good
relationships is a vital life skill. Recognizing the
value of relationships, effective communication
skills, and dispute resolution for older teenagers.

UNDERSTANDING THE IMPORTANCE OF
RELATIONSHIPS:

- Building connections: Relationships assist
  older kids to create connections with
  others and form a sense of community.

- Emotional support: Relationships give
  emotional support and may enable older
  teenagers to deal with stress and
  challenging circumstances.

- Personal growth: Relationships may assist older kids to learn more about themselves and acquire crucial life skills such as empathy and compromise.

EFFECTIVE COMMUNICATION SKILLS:

- Active listening: Practice active listening by giving full attention to the person speaking and responding wisely.

- Expressing oneself clearly: Learn how to communicate oneself clearly and assertively, without being violent.

- Understanding nonverbal communication: Learn to read and interpret nonverbal communication such as body language and facial expressions.

- Respecting limits: Learn to respect boundaries and communicate in a manner that is acceptable for the context and the relationship.

CONFLICT RESOLUTION: Understanding the Cause of Conflict:

- Identify the fundamental cause: It is necessary to understand the underlying causes of the dispute to successfully settle it.

- Take responsibility: Take responsibility for one's behaviors and emotions, and attempt to understand how they may have contributed to the dispute.

ACTIVE LISTENING:

- Listen actively: Pay complete attention to the other person and attempt to comprehend their viewpoint.

- Avoid interrupting: Avoid interrupting or talking over the other person, and let them express themselves fully.

- Reflect: Reflect on what the other person has stated to indicate that you have heard and grasped their viewpoint.

FINDING COMMON GROUND:

- Look for common ground: Identify areas of agreement and strive to create a solution that fits the requirements of both sides.

- Focus on the issue, not the person: Try to remove the individual from the issue, and concentrate on finding a solution.

- Be open-minded: Be open-minded and eager to explore diverse options.

SEEKING HELP:

- Identify a neutral third party: If required, seek support from a neutral third party such as a teacher, counselor, or mediator.

- Follow up: Follow up after the dispute has been settled to confirm that the solution is functioning and that both parties are happy.

CHAPTER 9

INDEPENDENT LIVING SKILLS

As older teenagers start to take on more responsibility and freedom, developing key life skills for independent living is critical. In this chapter, we will examine preparation for independent living, fundamental life skills, and problem-solving and decision-making for older teenagers.

PREPARING FOR INDEPENDENT LIVING:

- Setting objectives: Set realistic goals for independent living and build a strategy to attain them.

- Budgeting: Learn how to budget and manage money successfully.

- Time management: Learn how to manage time efficiently to balance duties and leisure activities.

- Self-care: Learn how to take care of oneself, both physically and psychologically.

ESSENTIAL LIFE SKILLS:

- Cooking: Learn how to create easy and healthful meals.

- Cleaning: Learn how to maintain a clean and orderly living place.

- Laundry: Learn how to do laundry and iron garments.

- Basic house repairs: Learn how to conduct basic home repairs such as replacing a light bulb or unclogging a drain.

PROBLEM-SOLVING AND DECISION-MAKING:

- Identifying the issue: Identify the problem and collect information to comprehend the situation.

- Generating choices: Generate various options for addressing the issue.

- Evaluating choices: Evaluate the options and evaluate the merits and disadvantages of each one.

- Making a choice: Make a decision and take action to execute the answer.

By preparing for independent living, gaining critical life skills, and developing problem-solving and decision-making abilities, older teens may take charge of their lives and be more ready to face the difficulties and responsibilities of living alone.

CHAPTER 10

CIVIC ENGAGEMENT AND SOCIAL RESPONSIBILITY

Civic involvement and social responsibility are vital for developing strong and healthy communities. It is the active engagement of residents in the political, social, and economic growth of their community.

By becoming involved and responsible citizens, people may have a positive effect on the lives of others and strive towards building a better society for everyone.

Volunteering and community service are fundamental kinds of civic involvement. They enable people to give back to their community and make a difference in the lives of others.

Not only do they aid others, but they also equip volunteers with essential skills and experiences, as well as a feeling of purpose and pleasure.

By helping, older kids may learn about the needs and difficulties of their community, and gain a greater grasp of social concerns.

To increase social awareness and responsibility, older teenagers may also educate themselves on current events and social problems, join political campaigns and advocacy organizations, and engage in conversations and debates with their classmates and community members. This may help kids develop critical thinking abilities, create their perspectives, and take a more active part in influencing the world around them.

One option for older kids to become active in civic participation and social responsibility is through volunteering with local groups that correspond with their interests and beliefs. This might involve working with organizations, schools, or community centers. They may also join in community service initiatives, such as cleaning up local parks, organizing food drives, or mentoring young children.

Older teenagers may also start their efforts to address social problems they care about.

Whether it's organizing a charity event, developing a community garden, or starting a youth-led advocacy campaign, there are numerous ways to have a good effect on the community.

In conclusion, civic involvement and social responsibility are crucial for developing strong and healthy communities. By being involved and responsible citizens, older teenagers may have a positive influence on the lives of others and strive towards building a better society for everyone.